THE SEARCH FOR IDENTITY IN EMILY BRONTE'S WUTHERING HEIGHTS AND POEMS

THE SELF IN IDENTITY FORMATION

DR. SAMPA CHATTERJEE

Dedicated to

My Teachers at Ealing College of Higher Education,

(now West London University), London, U.K

Contents

Preface   *vii*

Acknowledgements   *xi*

1. The Question Of Personal Identity   1

2. Wuthering Heights   8

3. Poems   18

4. Conclusion : 'In Love With The Absolute'   31

Cited Works   39

Preface

The Search for Identify is a theme which has fascinated me over the years. It has been a natural inclination of mine to look however tentatively it may be, at different literary works in the light of this theory. The search in the case of Emily Bronte invites rewarding research touching upon areas of philosophy, psychology and mysticism.

This is not simply the Identity sought by the Individual in society, nor is it a conflict between man and social environment as we find in modern writings. It is Identity sought in some 'transcendentalism'. In the first chapter we find a general discussion on 'Identity in childhood' later developing into an importance of the 'self' and fear of 'ego-loss' which in turn gives way to something higher - when the Individual forgets his own 'self' to find fulfilment in some 'Other' being. Sometimes this sort of Identity is even sought in death or after death, as Death is not supposed to be considered as a waste of human life but merely a shift into a different phase or chamber of Existence, and the Identity which is established is wholly spiritual leading one to believe in the immortality of the soul. This discussion is mainly based on the theory of Erik H. Erikson to whose extensive research on 'Identity' (Childhood and society, 1950), I am deeply indebted, and in this context, I have also tried my best to cite supporting examples from the works of Freud, Starbuck, Hindu philosophy and common theories set forth by popular philosophy and religion of various periods.

In the second and third chapters of my book I have related incidents and ideas of the novel **Wuthering Heights** and poems to this theory of Identity formation and have shown how Identity can really be sought in some 'otherness' and that everything may not meet with total disintegration and destruction in Death.

Identity formation in **Wuthering Heights** is identified with the rocky, desolate moorland in the novel. Heathcliff cries out after Catherine's death - "Be with me always - take any form -drive me mad! only do not leave me in this abyss, where I cannot find you! oh, God! it is unutterable! I cannot live without my life! I cannot live without my soul!" (Bronte 169) Caterine's spirit haunts the moors, her appearance as a glost child to Mr. Lockwood, the narrator of the novel's frame seems to reflect her 'life-after death', one who has lost her way and wants to be let inside Wuthering Heights, it is her unhappy search for 'the self', search for the person, who is the owner of the house - Mr. Heathcliff. Catherine remains bound to Wuthering Heights as a second kind of haunting presence through Heathcliff's own projection of her image in none but him. Heathcliff associates her with images that exist outside and beyond her, in nature, other people, Wuthering Heights, and himself. Heathcliff finds himself - surrounded with her image, the figural identification that he finds in "every cloud, in every tree" emphasize an uncanny connection with Catherine wherever he is, all the time, everywhere. He calls for the reader's pity for his alienation in the world around him, as well as a wonder and appreciation to find an identity much beyond the social order and it is only in death that unification of the 'self' is perhaps possible and identity formation is complete, far away from social constraints and finally realize the fantasy of a harmonious 'wholeness' or 'completeness'.

The conclusion is an attempt to understand Emily Bronte's personal life and mental state mainly, in order to bring out what actually could have led her to seek her 'Identity' in a markedly different way from most of the writers of her time.

Acknowledgements

This book owes its heartfelt gratitude to all who have inspired me in the process and have shown their concern in my effort. I am indebted to the Libraries of West London University, the British Council Division Kolkata and last but not the least to Notion Press Publishers for their co-operation and sincere wishes.

Special thanks goes to my son Somjit and my husband Dr Muktinath Chatterjee for their technical support in the making of the book.

WUTHERING HEIGHTS

A NOVEL,

BY

ELLIS BELL,

IN THREE VOLUMES.

VOL. I.

LONDON:

THOMAS CAUTLEY NEWBY, PUBLISHER,
72, MORTIMER St., CAVENDISH Sq.

1847.

I

The Question of Personal Identity

The questions 'who am I?' or 'for what am I?' are haunting impulses on the plane of existence. The search for this Identity constitutes a major theme in the philosophy of Existentialism, specially in the works of J. P. Sartre and some other stalwarts of Literature and in the history of man in general. In psychology, religion and literature also it has been one of the popular themes.

The passionate striving of man for individuality in society and its consequences and implications acquired a decisive importance in the Literature of the Nineteenth Century. Among women novelists, Jane Austen (early Nineteenth Century) Charlotte Bronte and other writers have written novels on this theme. In Emily Bronte however, this acquires a new dimension -the search for Identity is not merely the 'Social identity', but it is the passion to lose the 'self' in some 'otherness', either in complete identification with another person or by absorption into nature. Apparently, it results in a waste of human lives for it is impossible for two persons to 'be' each other without destruction of the physical limitations that individualise and separate. This attempt to make what is 'outside' oneself identical with what is 'inside' oneself can only be possible in physical and human terms through 'death'. This work is an exploration of this intricate problem, its complications and consequences on the plane of existence in the context of one important English woman writer, Emily Bronte.

This search for identity can be traced down to childhood and according the psychologists like Freud, a child who has just been able to walk, seems to repeat the act for the pure delight of functioning and to master and perfect a newly initiated function. He becomes aware of the new status and stature of 'one who is able to walk'. In this, children cannot be fooled by condescending praise or encouragement; their ego-identity gains real strength only from whole hearted recognition of real accomplishment. If a child is deprived of all the forms of expression which permit him to develop and to integrate the next step in his identity, he defends it with an astonishing strength encountered in animals who are suddenly forced to defend their lives. The child even over manipulates himself, forms a precocious conscience and tries to gain power by stubborn control. He may even grow 'neurotic' in doing so.

Philosophy assumes that human conscience remains partially infantile throughout life and this is the core of human tragedy. The strength acquired at a particular stage is tested by the necessity to transcend it in such a way that the individual can take chances in the next stage with what was most vulnerably precious in the previous one. There is a philosophical belief that in the process of Identity, the first birth of the individual is into his own little world. Starbuck has said that 'at this stage the universe is organized around his own personality.' Then comes a disturbance in 'self-preservation' and 'self-enlargement' which results in the shifting of the field of consciousness from lower to higher bench, with a consequent removal of interest from the subject to an object - the beginning of the process of transcendence. This unselfing or 'conversion' (terms used by Starbuck) is often a new revelation. The person emerges from a limited world of existence into a larger world of being - a love for the 'absolute'. It is so real that in comparison the normal world of past perception seems but twilight at the best. To support his psychological argument, Freud himself takes the help of a philosophical discussion - "what I have in mind is, of course, the theory which Plato put into the mouth of Aristophanes in the Symposium, and which deals not only with the origin of the sexual instinct but also with the most important of its variations in relation to its object. The original human nature was not like the present, but different. In the first place, the sexes were originally three in number, not two as they are now, there was man, woman, and the union of the two. Everything about these primaeval men was double; they had four hands and four feet, two faces, two privy parts and so on. Eventually Zeus decided to cut these men into two, 'like a sorb apple which is halved for pickling.' After the division had been made, 'the two parts of man each desiring his other half, came together and threw their arms about one another eager to grow into one." [1] Freud.

Freud in his **Beyond the Pleasure Principle**[2] has added this footnote: "I have to thank Professor Heinrich Gomperz of Vienna for the following discussion on the origin of the platonic myth which I give partly in his own words.

It is to be noted that what is essentially the same theory is also to be found in Hinduism and in the Upanishads. For we find the following passage in the Brihadaranyaka Upanishad, 1.4.3. [Max Muller's translation, 2, 85] where the origin of the world from the Atman (the Self or Ego) is described: "But he felt no delight. Therefore, a man who is lonely feels no delight. He wished for a second. He was so large as man and wife together. He then made this his self to fall in two, and then arose husband and wife. Therefore, Yajnavalkya said, "We two are thus (each of us) like half a shell."

Here we are also aware of the divine truth in Hindu Philosophy where Brahma creates Beings and Himself is present in all as, there is also a desire in all Beings to be one with the Supreme Being – Brahma. In this context of the fusion of one's identity with that of another, we may say that there is one constant fact which is true of all poets and all times – the discovery of oneself depends on an act of 'submission'. For the poets, as for human beings, to lose one's life is to find it.

This power of seeing one in another has also been analyzed by Freud who says " ... it may be difficult, too, for many of us, to abandon the belief that there is an instinct towards perfection at work in human beings, which has brought them to their present high level of intellectual achievement and ethical sublimation and which may be expected to watch over their development into superman" (Ibid. Page 36).

He goes on to say – "I have no faith, however, in the existence of any such internal instinct and I cannot see how this benevolent illusion is to be preserved …. what appears in a minority of individuals as an untiring impulsion towards further perfection can easily be understood as a result of the instinctual repression upon which is based all that is most precious in human civilization …. and it is the difference in amount between the pleasure of satisfaction which is 'demanded' and that which is actually achieved that provides the driving factor which will permit of no halting at any position attained but in the poet's words, 'presses over forward unsubdued. - Mephistopheles In Faust I (Ibid. Page 36)

Whatever it is, the avoidance of such an experience (of finding one in another) because of a far of ego-loss may lead to a deep sense of isolation and self-absorption. This is also signified by a fear of death. Again, only when identity formation is well on its way that true intimacy is possible. The youth who is not sure of his own identity shies away or throws himself into acts of intimacy which are promiscuous without true fusion or real self-abandon. It is only the deep and ardent passion for a perceived object of love can persuade one to the act of abnegation, by which he kills his lesser love of desire and emerges into a new and higher world of existence. Again "Loss of love and failure leave behind them a permanent injury to self-regard in the form of a narcissistic scar, which in my opinion, as well as in Marcinkowski's (1918), contributes more than anything to the 'sense of inferiority' which is so common in neurotics." (Ibid pp.14-15).

In this state of transition, as Evelyn Underhill has said, that there is moral and mental disorder in men. Everything goes wrong with them. They are tormented by evil thoughts and abrupt temptations, lose grasp of their spiritual and worldly affairs. The soul experiences a 'dark night' when the self which thought itself to be so spiritual, so firmly established upon the super sensual plane, is forced to turn back, to leave the height, and again pick up the qualities which it had left behind. [3]

From this it is but natural to think that life is a constant struggle which culminates in death resulting in a sense of waste but, if we can take Freud's saying as a truth that everything living dies for 'internal' reasons - becomes inorganic once again - then we can conclude that 'the aim of life is death' and that 'inanimate things existed before living ones'. (Ibid.p.32). This show that Death is after all not a waste of human emotions and passions, rather it is a fulfillment of life. That is, one's 'identity' is only complete when man completes his journey from birth to death, or he finds his identity through Death.

Chapter References

1. Jowett's Translation
2. Translated and newly edited by James Strachey, London, 1961, pp. 51-52
3. Evelyn Underhill : **Mysticism**, London, 1911

II
Wuthering Heights

Emily Bronte (1818 - 1848) was far advanced of her age - we shall see from her works that she was not only a pioneer of the modern psychological novel, but has proved in later ages to be a powerful religious teacher, a philosopher and a psychologist besides being a literary artist of high merit.

From the records of the Brontes, it is known that Mr. Patrick Bronte, her father had literary ambitions in his youth and published in Bradford and neighbouring towns prose tales, poems, pamphlets and sermons. [1] His wife, Maria Branwell, before her marriage wrote with a view to publication in some periodical an essay entitled 'On the advantages of Poverty in Religious concerns.' Thus, it is not unnatural that the parents encouraged their children in self-culture. It is also known that they subscribed to a circulating library in the nearest town. However, Mr. Bronte as a father was stern and dominant. Moreover, a strict aunt and a lack of suitable young society had thrown the Bronte sisters entirely on their own devices for solace and amusements. The 'purple heather', the pale, tough and grass and the bold sweeping contours of the moors, where they spent most of their lives offered an aesthetic pleasure which moulded their taste to a great extent and provided a moral inspiration.

Emily Bronte was the tallest among her sisters and beautiful with kind, kindling eyes; but she was the loneliest person in the house because she was too reserved and a difficult person to converse with; She was content to dream and imagine in her own little world into which none had an access, she seemed to dwell in a privacy of her own and disliked people who would disturb her and try to bring her to the forefront. An extract from her Birthday Note which was written only when she was twenty seven expresses thus: "… I am quite contented for myself: not as idle as formerly, altogether as hearty, and having learnt to make the most of the present and long for the future with the fidgetiness that I cannot do all I wish; seldom or ever troubled with nothing to do and merely desiring that everybody could be as comfortable as myself and as undesponding and then we should have a very tolerable world of it….." [2] Again, her sister Charlotte Bronte writes of Emily Bronte in her letter to Ellen Nussey in 1848. "… she is too intractable I do wish I knew her state and feelings more clearly…" [3] Emily Bronte had no time for letter-writing like her sister Charlotte. Friendship and social functions were trivial to her; she was one of those reserved, uncommunicative beings who do not like to be questioned. Quite obviously, this mental disposition found expression in her works, especially in **Wuthering Heights** which was published after many obstructions (1847) at the hands of the press and publishers. More unbearable for a sensitive person were the reviews which followed one after another. Emily Bronte who had long cherished the dream of becoming an author one day, endured the criticisms with her natural poise and loftiness of heart.

The Self in Identity Formation:

To cite examples of criticisms of Wuthering Heights we may quote one or two passages of Nineteenth Century criticisms which are collected by Miriam Allott and are included in his edition of **The Brontes: The Critical Heritage**. [4] G.K. Peck in an unsigned review [5] of the novel had remarked: "It does not depict men and women guided merely by motives intelligible to simplest observers. It lifts the veil and shows boldly the dark side of our deployed nature." Again, Emile Montegut in an article [6] has said:" Wuthering Heights is the story of an irresistible passion...... But Heathcliff: he and she (Catherine) are, so to speak, but a single person; together they form a hybrid monster, twin-sexed and twin-souled; he is the male soul of the monster, she the female." Thus, the critics seemed to find in the novel nothing but a horror of great darkness brooding over it. Here, the modern reader will probably differ and be inclined to prove that there is nothing monstrous or diabolic about **Wuthering Heights**, and Heathcliff, but only a web of psychological actions in it. Emily Bronte was against the conventional ideas of love and religion, but from her works, it can be found that she was deeply religious in feeling, believed in an all-loving, Eternal Power who pitied human transgressions and granted rest in the end to all Sinners. Emily Bronte was revolted by the Methodist view of evil and the doctrine of eternal punishment, here she proved herself to be a rebel, an individualist, and her religion was an affair between herself and God - and this is best revealed in **Wuthering Heights**.

Apparently, Heathcliff is stormy, hard and unsocial - but if the critics would probe further into the character, they could find a good soul twisted and turned into evil by people and circumstances, especially when he nears his end, the spell of suffering being lifted from his shoulders. It has been already discussed in the First Chapter, that the stepping stone in the process of identity - formation is childhood. It is absolutely clean from the account of Nelly Dean that Heathcliff, from the time he has been brought to the family is ill-used and deprived of all expressions, neglected, insulted, treated worse than a servant. When Mr. Earnshaw brings him home, "Mrs. Earnshaw was ready to fling it out of doors" and "he seemed a sullen, patient child, hardened, perhaps to ill treatment; he could stand Hindley's blow without winking or shedding a tear". [7] Naturally, he soon grows to defend himself, becomes stubborn and over manipulates himself, when attempts are made to rob him of his 'ego-identity' he snatches it back and clings to it almost with a savage passion. He cannot be fooled by empty praise and sympathy; he refuses to shake hands with even Catherine, - his only oasis in that desert - "I shall not" he says, "I shall not stand to be laughed at. I shall not bear it." He goes on to tell Catherine "You needn't have touched me ... I shall be as dirty as I please: and I like to be dirty, and I will be dirty". (Ibid.p.58).

Heathcliff, turns almost neurotic on the eve of Catherine's marriage to Edgar Linton and loss of love and failure enhances his sense of inferiority. He runs away from Wuthering Heights and suffers from extreme loneliness perhaps, and it may be due to this, that his love for Catherine becomes more intense and gradually he undergoes the process of 'Conversion' or 'Unselfing' - he no longer seeks his identity in himself, but in Catherine - this is either Freud's instinct towards perfection, or Plato's transcendental philosophy, where man emerges from his own world of existence into a larger world of being - the passion for the absolute, in which man loses his own identity to find it in another. But this spiritual realization is only possible when there is no fear of ego loss or, when 'Identity formation' is well on its way. Thus, Heathcliff again proves to be a failure because his identity formation was hindered in childhood. Unable to give expression to his high thoughts, we find his bitterness and rage hardening into relentless scheming to wreck the lives and capture the fortunes of both families - the Earnshaws and the Lintons. His promiscuous act of marrying Isabella is a result of his tortured self-esteem. Yet, he is not in reality the devil incarnate. It is unjust to conclude from the account of Nelly Dean who was after all, a simple minded, country woman, whose very intellectual short comings make for violent impressions and the use of crude similes. It is difficult for one to believe that Heathcliff has come from the infernal world when one hears him at the end of Catherine's death-bed. It is a divine power from within which helps him to get over his madness, he realizes that he cannot bear Catherine's absence (he only wanted to punish her because of her consent in marrying Edgar Linton) and cries out "Oh, Cathy! Oh, my life! how can I bear it?" - and " ... Catherine, you know that I could as soon forget you as my existence!" (Ibid., pp.141-142 ...) "You loved me - then what right had you to leave me? What right - answer me - for the poor fancy you felt for Linton?

Because misery and degradation, and death, and nothing that God or Satan could inflict, would have parted us, you, of your own will, did it. I have not broken your heart - you have broken it; and in breaking it, you have broken mine … Do I want to live? … would you like to live with your soul in the grave? (Ibid. p. 144)" Catherine dies leaving Heathcliff in this stage of transition from the human to the superhuman plane. Identity formation is again checked and retarded and Heathcliff is forced to return to his former world of evil temptations and bitter sense of revenge. Again, he undergoes mental disorder and becomes unconscious of his deeds. Crushing the lives of the younger generation is the result of his losing this right of existence. Thus, he becomes responsible in making the child Linton grow up into a weak-willed young man, in making Hareton a brute and forcibly getting young Cathy married to his son. Yet these are not the conscious working of his soul. At the end, he recovers his sense when there is no more fear of losing anything, when he is about to be united with his Catherine. He is the least disturbed to find Hareton and Cathy as friends. "… I get levers and mattocks to demolish the two houses, and train myself to be capable of working like Hercules, and, when everything is ready and in my power … I don't care for striking, I can't take the trouble to raise my hand …. I have lost the faculty of enjoying their destruction, and I am too idle to destroy for nothing........." he tells Nelly Dean (Ibid. p.268). In Hareton he sees his own youth and his association with young Cathy reminds him of his past, he does not want to deprive the two of their identities - "Well, Hareton's aspect was the ghost of my immortal love; of my wild endeavours to hold my right; my degradation, my pride, my happiness, and my anguish." He struggles on to be united with his Catherine, he yearns to be one with her - "O God! It is a long fight; I wish it were over!" (Ibid. p.269). He is haunted by this single idea and finally dies and attains his Identity in being united with his beloved in the grave.

Catherine however, is not neglected or tortured in childhood like Heathcliff. Rather she is given too much attention. But she is gifted with the divine equality of love and it is through this love that she seeks to be united and become one with Heathcliff. Her purpose in marrying Linton is to make Heathcliff rise in society. To her, marriage is not the only culmination of love. Love to her is Religion which cannot be altered or done away with by any human law. When Nelly Dean is bewildered at her marrying Edgar Linton and talking of her love for Heathcliff at the same time, she exclaims "If all else perished and he remained, I should still continue to be, and if all else remained and he were annihilated, the universe would turn to a mighty stranger. I should not be a part of it ... Nelly, I am Heathcliff: So, don't talk of our separation again" (Ibid.p.81). She is not given enough scope to express her feelings in childhood, nobody understands her and she is thrown into isolation and it is this isolation that nourishes the noble sentiments that were hidden in her. Her marriage to Linton precipitates her union with Heathcliff. She tells Heathcliff "I wish I could hold you, till we are both dead: ... I only wish us never to be parted; and should a word of mine distress you hereafter, think I feel the same distress underground, and for my own sake, forgive me ..." (Ibi.p.142). Catherine cannot dream of any evil in her being one with Heathcliff. Therefore, when she nears her end, she wants Heathcliff by her side, she sees herself in him "Oh, don't don't go! It is the last time! Edgar will not hurt us, Heathcliff, I shall die! I shall die!" (Ibid.p.145)

Apparently, this sort of Identity cannot be attained in life owing to physical limitations and it is only possible through death - thus resulting in a waste of life. Here again, if one has gone through the First Chapter of this book, he will become aware of the human instinct craving for perfection, for being a superman. What is required is the exertion of this instinct and for this, proper guidance in the most formative period of life' - that is childhood, is wanted. This later, helps him to become aware of his existence in the world and it is then that, he can emerge from the limited world of sense into the larger world of 'Being' - that is the 'Absolute'. Even if this sort of Identity is possible through death, death as we have come to know is not a waste of human life; it is rather a fulfillment of life as Freud believes and that life and death are both natural occurrences on the plane of existence. At the end of **Wuthering Heights**, when Catherine is dead, to Heathcliff she continues to be present in all things animate and inanimate - "The entire world is a dreadful collection of memoranda that she did exist, and that I have lost her! Well, Hareton's aspect was the ghost of my immortal love; of my wild endeavours to hold my right." (Ibid.p.269). The lover left on earth seeks union with the beloved even in the grave and he attains it; for Emily Bronte has not merely grasped the modern idea of the supreme value of the individual soul, where "There is no room for Death, Nor atom that his might should render void" (Emily Bronte's poem **No Coward Soul is Mine**!)- but also realizes itself in its personal life and in mutual understanding, complete harmony, virtual identity with its destined mate; she seems the personality and the consummated union as eternal facts, which mortality itself cannot destroy.

Nelly Dean only stands as a mouthpiece for conventional ideas about the Nineteenth Century gender and social class; according to her, Catherine's 'unfeminine' part of herself defies gendered expectations as she rejects the stereotyped upper-class girlhood to the, wild, aggressive, untamable, 'unfeminine' sense of self and remains socially alienated mentally throughout. In fact, both Catherine and Heathcliff share the trauma of alienation from the social sphere. Thus, both seem to disrupt the morality in the social order and find refuge in a lonely 'inhuman world' and remain the children of rock, health and tempest, striving to find their identity in the creation of identity in their united 'Selves'. This kind of Imaginary Identity does not find a proper place in the existing social order. Though placed in a sophisticated social class of the Lintons and undergoing the flashes of a refined culture of a higher social order, the inner conflict of Catherine, torn between the two worlds of Edgar Linton and Heathcliff cannot be overlooked and thrown aside; her identity-formation is twisted and thwarted as 'Heathcliff is inseparably connected in her mind with her beloved moors beyond society'. Their suffering in the process of identity formation is traumatic, a fragmented identity that only meets fulfillment and completion in their union through death.

Chapter References

1. This and the following biographical information are derived from Irene Cooper Willis's **The Brontes: Great Lives, London, 1933**.

2. Emily Bronte's Birthday Note dt. 30th July, 1945 included in **The Bronte Letters, ed. Muriel Spark, London & New York, 1954, p.121**.

3. Ibid., pp. 155-56.

4. **The Brontes: The Critical Heritage, ed. Miriam Allott, London, 1974**.

a. **American Review, Jan. 1848 vii. 572-85**. Included in Allott's edition ed. cited, p.240.
b. Dated 1st July 1857, tome 4, 139-84 included in Allott's edition ed. cited p.377.

5. **Wuthering Heights**: Penguin Books, England, First published 1847, published in Penguin Books 1946, 10th report, 1964, pp.45-66. All subsequent quotations of the novel are taken from this edition.

III
Poems

The poems of Emily Bronte reveal almost the same philosophical insight that we find in her novel **Wuthering Heights**. The view that identity can be sought in some 'other self' or in 'some otherness' seems to be more well established here and reflects a more strong belief and firmness than is found in **Wuthering Heights**. It is characterized by "a calm of mind all passion spent". (1) Here the psychological argument is strongly supported by mysticism. In **Wuthering Heights**, the protagonists are led astray when proper ego-integration is hampered and suffers the 'dark night of the soul'. At the end they find their identities in each other through death which they consider to be the beginning of a new life. The same struggle in the poems is somewhat less intense, the realization is more deep and passion and emotion are poised by a sound belief in oneself and some other higher power.

It was Charlotte Bronte who first came across the poems in 1846, and edited them. It was she who first got a glimpse into Emily Bronte's secret life behind that silence and reserve which she showed everyone in the world. In this year there appeared a 'slim volume of verse' which sold two copies. With the title **Poems of Currer, Ellis and Acton Bell** it represented the first venture of the Bronte Sisters into publishing and included twenty-one poems by Emily Bronte. A further eighteen by her were published in the 1850 volume which Charlotte edited after Anne's and Emily's deaths. Since then, larger editions of her poems have come out culminating in G.W. Hatfield's **Complete Poems of Jane Emily Bronte** which appeared in 1941 and included one hundred and ninety-three pieces, either complete or in fragment form.

Here, I shall consider an important current of thought which Emily Bronte entertained in her verse - a form of personal quietism which places her on a more higher level than being a mere poet of pessimism. The cry for liberty and the constant struggle to assert and reassert her identity in her loneliness aches throughout all her poems.

'Leave the heart that now I bear,

And give me liberty....'

'No Coward Soul is Mine'are her sayings; but it is with difficulty that she trusted even that message of life which she seemed to discover in death. She has to assure herself of it again and again: 'who once lives, never dies...'

Considering such trends of thought critics have also recognized the influence of the Romantic poets on Emily Bronte's work. Muriel Spark in her edition [2] of Emily's poems, reckons the influences as principally seven; the Border Balladists, Cowper, Burns, Wordsworth, Byron and

Scott, and Seventeenth Century lyricists. In her desire to escape from the world around herself into a higher world of thought she undoubtedly resembles the Romantics. Yet there is something more in her poems besides a sense of escape. Her ego-identity is thwarted in her real world; therefore, she seeks her identity and yearns to become one with 'something else'. It is not merely the feeling of being along with the 'Skylark' of Shelley, or the 'Nightingale' of Keats. but it is the feeling of finding the self in that 'otherness itself':

> *Though earth and moon were gone,*
> *And suns and universe ceased to be*
> *And Thou wert left alone,*
> *Every Existence would exist in Thee*

(No Coward Soul is Mine)

It is somewhat the same philosophy of the metaphysical poet John Donne. In **The Good Morrow** of Donne one identity blends in another:

> *'Let sea-discoverers to new worlds have gone,*
> *Let maps to other worlds on worlds have shown*
> *Let us possess one world, each hath one, and is one" and*
> *again -*
> *"My face in thine eyes, thine in mine appears*
> *And true plain hearts do in the faces rest,*
>
> ...
>
> *Whatever dies was not mixed equally;*
> *If our two loves be one, or thou and I*
> *Love so alike that none do slacken, none can die"* [3]

Only Donne seems to us more earthly, whereas Emily Bronte appears to be more a mystic and religious teacher, than a social reformer that we find in Charlotte Bronte -

> *"So if a tear, when thou art dying,*
> *Should haply fall from me,*
> *It is not that my soul is sighing*
> *To go and rest with thee"*

(Emily Bronte in her **Stanzas**)

It was not mere passion that tempted her in writing these lines. In referring to her personal life, we find critics mentioning her love affair with a particular Rev. Mr. Weightman but as E.A. Baker suggests, there is no concrete proof - it is mere assumption and no particular person was the object of her lament. She was a mystic by natural disposition and her ideas were completely original.

Discussing her mental set up and extraordinary ideas, Rover Wilson [5] says that Childhood played an important role in her life. Being extremely sensitive, any painful memory cast an everlasting impression on her from which she found difficult to release herself. Aunt Branwell's misguided attempt to correct Emily and shutting her up one afternoon in the room where Mrs. Bronte had died, unhappiness at being temporarily away from the moors when she was sent to school, the absence of her mother all enhanced her loneliness.

Neglect, real or imaginary made her hard, black and morose at least in her own fancy; enormous pride glorifying in enormous loneliness. It is obvious for impetuous spirits of her kind to ask for quick and perhaps violent response to their emotions. They are, easily, deeply wounded, easily feel shame and what is worse imagine 'neglect' to them - the most intolerable thing on earth. In a letter to Ellen Nussey in 1848 Charlotte Bronte writes of Emily Bronte ".... she is too intractable. I do wish I know her state and feelings more clearly...."[6]

Prison is the theme of much of her poetry but although she weeps in solitary rooms her pride does not allow her to accept defeat - there is a constant effort to seek identity even if it is attained through death:

The Prisoner

A Fragment

St.1 : In the dungeon crypts idly did I stray

Reckless of the lives wasting these away,

St.5 : The Captive raised her hand and

pressed it to her brow;

'I have been struck', She said,

'and I am suffering now';

Yet these are little worth, your bolts

and irons strong

And, were they forged in steel, they

could not hold me long.

St. 15 : Yet I should lose no sting, would

Wish no torture less;

The more that anguish racks, the

earlier it will bless,

And robed in fires of hell, or bright

with heavenly shine

If it but herald death the

vision is divine.'

It is the picture of a fear of ego-loss. The sense of personal identity which persist throughout all her poems is a sense, not of the delight, but of the pain and ineradicable sting of personal identity. Failing to find her identity in life, she seeks it through 'death', through the 'absolute truth', through the 'only perfection of life'. Thus begins the 'dark night' of the soul which leads to a more concrete and mature understanding gradually. The passion to lose the 'self' in some 'other person' (as is seen in **Wuthering Heights**) is overcome by the serenity to lose the 'self' in some 'divine power or death'. There is a defiance, a non-acceptance of life it seems. The mental disorder which often results in the case of normal human beings effecting an indulgence in evil temptations is suppressed by the deep love embedded in her soul.

It matters little to the poet if this identity is achieved through death : The last stanza in

Death

Strike it down, that other bough may flourish
Where that perished sapling used to be;
Thus, at least, its mouldering corpse will nourish
That from which it sprung - Eternity

'Emily' said Mrs. Gaskell, "must have been a remnant of the Titans, great grand-daughter of the giants who used to inhabit the earth." [7] In this respect Emily Bronte resembles Lord Byron to some extent.

How much Emily Bronte knew of the life of Byron is not known, but as F.B. Pinion suggests (8) her familiarity with Moore's biography is beyond doubt. It seems likely that, whether she realized it or not, she drew a number of suggestions from it for her novel and poems. They could include the resentment kindled by violent punishment in boyhood; a thwarted affection which induced thoughts of heartlessness and crime.

Mathew Arnold coupled their names in Howorth Churchyard :

SHE

(How shall I sing her?) whose soul
Knew no fellow for might,
Passion, Vehemence, grief,
Daring, since Byron died

But Critics like Romer Wilson in **All Alone**[9] had a great deal to say about the psychological influence of Byronism and the Byron legend on Emily Bronte, but not a word about his poetry - in fact did not regard him as an influence in the perfectly ordinary and straightforward way in which one poet is usually said to have influenced another. Her preoccupation with death is natural enough in a person whose mother died when she was three, and two elder sisters when she was six and also because her imagination was naturally gloomy, but it is not entirely satisfying one may feel that even the most tragic of imaginations must have been encouraged by 'something' in the external world to produce this orgy of guilt and misery. Whether that 'something' was the hell-fire preaching of 'Methodism' of which she must have heard much in her childhood, the mad Methodist magazines full of miracles and apparition and preternatural warnings, ominous dreams and frenzied fanaticism, [10] which Charlotte Bronte mentions in **Shirley** or whether it was the influence of Byron remains unsolved.

However, I feel these are chance similarities and Emily Bronte's ideas were completely original, she was a mystic by nature and was not influenced by Shelley but shared the transcendental belief or philosophy with him. Life, as she experienced it in her house was meaningful - She bent all her efforts towards defining this meaning, through the direct methods of her literary work, and by indirect means, which included her household and family duties. [11] In **The Philosopher** the desire to lose herself in some transcendental power is keenly felt. Failing to get identity in life, she now prepares herself for death :

THE PHILOSOPHER

2nd *Stanza : 'Oh, for the time when I shall sleep*

without Identity............'

And never care how rain may steep,

Or snow may cover me!

No promised heaven, these wild desires

Could all, or half fulfil;

No threatened hell, with quenchless fires

Subdue this quenchless will!'

3rd Stanza : So said I, and still say the same;

Still, to my death, will say -

Three Gods, within this little frame,

Are warring night and day;

Heaven could not hold them all, and yet

They all are held in me;

And must be mine till I forget

My present entity!

Oh for the time, when in my breast

Their struggles will be O'er

Oh, for the day, when I shall rest;

And never suffer more.

5th Stanza : And even for that spirit, seer,

I've watched and sought my life time long;

Sought him in heaven hell, earth, and aim,

And endless search, and always wrong

Had I but seen his glorious eye

Once light the clouds that wilder me;

I ne'er had raised this coward cry

To cease to think, and cease to be;

Death seems to her not a waste, but a new beginning. The pain at receiving a check on Identity - formation in her life (a note of which still lingers in **The Philosopher**) subsides gradually. Her health deteriorates and she prepares herself for the end with a philosophic calm with a satisfaction which is entirely her own.

Charlotte Bronte records the bitter progress of Emily Bronte's last week - to W.S. Williams: "She is a real stoic in illness. She neither seems nor will accept sympathy. To put any questions, to offer any aid, is to annoy; she will not yield a step before pain of sickness till forced; not one of her ordinary avocations will she voluntarily renounce. You must look on and see her do what she is obviously unfit to do, and not dare say a word - a painful necessity for those to whom her health and existence are as precious as the life in their veins". We find in -

THE NIGHT WIND

Last Stanza : 'There truly, when that breast is cold

Thy prisoned soul shall rise;

The dungeon mingle with the mould -

The captive with the skies.

Nature's deep being , thine shall hold,

Her spirit all thy spirit fold,

Her breath absorb thy sighs.

Mortal! though soon life's tale is told,

Who once lives, never dies!'

*And this belief grows more intense when she ultimately
finds this sort of identity in -*

There is no room for death,

Nor atom that his might could render void

Thou, - thou art Being and Breath,

And what thou art may never be destroyed -

(No Coward Soul is Mine)

Robin Grove writes of Emily Bronte's poems - "But to
return to the poems, I do not know that she achieved a
comparable equipoise there ..." [12] It is quite impossible to
accept such criticism about a person who has acquired

the vision of a mystic, who has conquered the pains of Death (no matter with how much effort and struggle) and who has gone beyond it to see in it another beginning - To whom Death is not a waste, perfection will come naturally and he or she is bound to achieve calmness or equipoise and this exactly is reflected in Emily Bronte's poems. Apparently, the tone of the poems may be pessimistic, bearing a sense of depression and loss, but she does not leave us there - she finds a reason for enjoying life to the brim as she finds a sort of 'existence' even in death.

REFERENCES

1. John Milton: **Samson Agonistes**, ed. F.T. Prince, OUP, 1957, reprt. 1977. line 1758.

2. Muriel Spark and D. Stanford: **Emily Bronte her life and work**, London, 1960, fifth impression, 1975.

3. **The Metaphysical Poets** : Selected and edited by Helen Gardner, Penguin Books, 1957, reprt. 1961. p.56.

4. E.A. Baker : **The History of the English Novel**, 10 vols. 1937, Vol.8.

5. Romer Wilson: **All Alone The Life and Private History of E.J. Bronte**, London, 1928.

6. **The Bronte Letters** ed. M. Spark, ed. cited, pp. 155-56, 1954, University of Oklahoma

7. E.A. Baker : **The History of the English Novel** ed. cited Vol.8, Chapter XXVII, p.70, 1934, footnote.

8. F.B. Pinion : **A Bronte Companion**, London, 1975.

9. Romer Wilson : **All Alone - The Life and Private History of E.J. Bronte**, ed. cited. Chatto & Windus, 1928

10. **The Influence of Byron on E. Bronte** - an article by Helen Brown, included in **The Modern Language Review** ed. Charles J. Sisson, William J. Entwistle and A.G. Atkins, Vol. 34, 1939.

11. M. Spark and D. Stanford : **Emily Bronte her life and work**, ed. cited, p.11. Peter Owen, 1960

12. **The Art of Emily Bronte** ed. Anne Smith, London, 1976. The Particular article is by Robin Grove entitled **It would not do** Emily Bronte as Poet, p.51.

IV
Conclusion : 'In Love with the Absolute'

Thus, it is not the Identity Sought by Charles Dickens in the Victorian age focusing the Individual against Society, nor is it a struggle of Jane Eyre for a place of the woman in society, it is something more personal, something more Romantic in outlook; it is a blend of philosophy, psychology and mysticism and in this we find no more physical struggle, on the other hand, we discover that the struggle is more mental to seek identity in some 'other person' or some 'otherness' and 'the sense of waste' which results from it - if it results at all, for this 'Identity formation' as seen sometimes culminates in Death and in life after Death.

In fact to Emily Bronte, 'Death' was not an end, but a 'new beginning' as she herself believed and looked forward to. It was a vision she saw perhaps which could have been her secret. This however gets reflected in her works and it is evident that the Identity which she seeks is somewhat spiritual. Charles Morgan in his article [1] on Emily Bronte has referred to Miss Mary Sinclair's suggestion of Emily Bronte being of the company of Blake, not indeed in manner nor in faith, but in her capacity for spiritual absolution, Miss Sinclair speaks of her as having been "in love with the Absolute" and we need not seek any phrase which is perhaps more apt. She adds that Emily "was a mystic not by religious vocation, but by temperament and the ultimate vision" and that none can comprehend her genius who does not himself with "passion and sincerity", embrace the idea of "the illusory nature of time and of material happenings" [1]. This also could not have been better said.

As Emily Bronte felt the life of earth to be the only source of redeeming attraction during man's mortal existence, so she feels that the life of earth even after the individual's death is still man's final consolation. Earth appears as a mourner for mankind, since men must die; but even so, says she, their death does not deprive the death of man's affection, since their last wish is for an earthy hereafter, a prolongation of spatial existence beyond the state of temporal impermanence. Man then, she seems to be saying, belongs to the earth both in life and in death; and one of the most harmonious moments which he can know are those wherein his own personality is suspended so that he is dead to himself, or to his own narrow identity by immersion in the greater life of nature.

The very fact that made her hide herself from publicity behind a pseudonym and expose herself to harsh criticism reveals to us that she was one of uncommon genius who was beyond mere temporal attractions. From Irene Cooper Willis' **The Brontes**[2] we come to know that "Emily was bitterly disappointed at the apparent failure of her novel. The rumour that it was by the author of Jane Eyre must have galled her, as also the change of tone in some later reviews as to the respective merits of the authors of the poems". This is confirmed by one of Charlotte Bronte's letters to Mr. Williams regarding the criticism of the Bells in the North American Review. "Ellis" she wrote, "the man of uncommon talents, but dogged, brutal and morose' sat leaning back in his easy chair, drawing his impeded breath as he best could not looking, also piteously pale and wasted: it is not his want to laugh, but he smiled, half amused and half in scorn, as he listened." Apparently, she may have seemed pale and wasted as she also embraced an early death, yet the very last words of this letter make her feel that she was looking forward to, or even may have discovered her recognition somewhere else, such beyond her own little 'self.' She wrote more for herself than for the public. Keats indeed expressed, on Emily Bronte's behalf as it were, the artistic attitudes which we know from her behavior to have been hers. She too could well have declared as he did in a letter to Reynolds of 9th April 1818 "I never wrote one single line of poetry with the least shadow of public thought", or again, "my imagination is a monastery, and I am its monk" (letter to Shelley, August 1820) who more than Emily Bronte felt able to "refuse the poisonous suffrage of a public" in the knowledge that "the soul is a world of itself, and has enough to do in its own home" (Keats' letter to Reynolds, 25th Aug. 1819). By the adoption of such attitudes implicit though inarticulate, Emily Bronte repels rather than invites critical attention discouraging any casual or trivial approaches to her work.

Turning once again to her background, we may get proof for this sort of temperament of hers. She had two lives. It was the essence of her genius that they were distinct. One, the superficial life, the life of the daughter at the parsonage, which she commonly praised for having led with dutiful heroism. It was the activity in the midst of which she had learned how to feed upon the spirit within her; she had an impenetrable reserve and had an extreme fondness of being lonely; she felt herself to be one with the lonely bleak moors; she had a rare and expressive look, something to remember through life and, which showed that she was trying to find herself in some other plane, beyond herself. Being tired of being enclosed, she was weary to escape to "that glorious world" (**Wuthering Heights**) of which perhaps, she had once enjoyed immediate apprehension. All her life, all her poems, all those sorts of Wuthering Heights that bear the stamp of vision were dedicated to her desire that, this direct experience might be repeated, that she might be again "really with it and in it - not seeing it dimly, through tears and yearning for it through the walls of an aching heart." (**Wuthering Heights**)

There are in the poems, indications enough that this experience, this achievement of the Absolute with which she was ever afterwards "in love" identified in her mind with an individuality known to be ghostly in its relation to the earthly plane, but having for her an unforgettable reality and probably an anthropomorphic form; she seemed to echo one single note in almost all her poems.

Thought followed thought, star followed star

Through boundless regions on;

While one sweet influence, near and far,

Thrilled through, and proved us one!" [3]

Death appeared to her in one aspect as an end of the blissful torture she would not have lessened, in another aspect, as a possible reversal of her failure - an opportunity to be "really with and in" the Supreme familiar spirit, she did not know whether to dread death as a cessation or to desire it as an opportunity. Yet if death would mean a total waste of human passions and emotions, it is certain that she did not want to die. "She was torn, conscious, panting reluctant, out of a happy life." Charlotte Bronte wrote to Ellen Nussey later. [4] "She knows for certain that even though all physical limitations would perish and be destroyed, man's identity would still exist in the spirit which is indestructible and immortal. Therefore, she could write -

"When I am not and none beside

Nor earth nor sea nor cloudless sky

But only spirit wandering wide

Through infinite immensity". [5]

Therefore, however critics may call this attitude of hers - a result of pessimism due to an unsuccessful life, I personally feel that she was much above the petty glamour and fascination of worldly fame; her yearning was for something more permanent and constructive and in this struggle she could not have failed - if she was not able to find an answer form 'the glorious world', she could not have made Catherine Earnshaw cry out - "I am Heathcliff" or "he's in my soul", and this reward to her was much more desirable than empty worldly praise. So in seeking a larger identity, she has been able to establish the fact that one can find oneself in another without any waste of human lives. Death temporarily parts men from each other to unite them elsewhere, or even if Death does not come, one can really 'be' another if he lifts himself, rather if he is spiritually advanced to renounce his physical 'self' and dissolve in the transcendental platonic world, which to him is the ideal world of perfection. There in his imagination, a realization becomes so intense that, he forgets himself and is engrossed and enwrapped with the personality of another.

I strongly assert that one can never, ever come to the conclusion that "a horror of great darkness" broods over **Wuthering Heights** as per existing criticism, rather I feel that it is a vision of the sublime in identity-search that reigns throughout the novel.

Chapter References

1. Charles Morgan : **"Emily Bronte"** An article included in The Great Victorians 2 vols. Pelican Books, ed. V.K. Krishna Menon, 1937, Vol.1. p.81.
2. Irene Cooper Willis : **The Brontes** ed. cited. pp. 126-127. Duckworth. 1936
3. **The Complete Poemsof Emily Jane Bronte** ed. Clement Shorter and C.W. Hatfield , Hodder & Stoughton1923, p.3.
4. Irene Cooper Willis - **The Brontes** ed. cited p. 135. Duckworth 1936
5. M. Spark and D. Stanford : **Emily Bronte : her life and work,** ed. cited, P-184. Peter Owen, 1960

CITED WORKS

1. Allot, Miriam ed. : **The Brontes** : The Critical Heritage, London, 1974.

2. Baker, E.A. : **The History of the English Novel**, 10 vols. 1950.

3. Bronte, Emily : **Wuthering Heights**, Penguin Books, 10th reprt. 1964.

4. Brown, Helen : **The Influence of Byron on Emily Bronte**" an article included in The Modern Language Review ed. Charles J. Sission, William J. Entwistle and A.G. Atkins, Vol. 34, 1939.

5. Freud, Sigmund : **Beyond The Pleasure Principle**, Translated and newly edited by James Strachey, London, 1961.

6. Gardner, Helen ed. : **The Metaphysical Poets**, Penguin Books, 1957 reprt. 1961.

7. Grove, Robin : "**It would not do**" Emily Bronte as Poet - an article included in The Art of Emily Bronte ed. Anne Smith, London, 1976.

8. Milton, John : **Samson Agonistes** ed. F.T. Prince, OUP, 1957, reprt.1977.

9. Morgan, Charles : "**Emily Bronte**" - an article included in **The Great Victorians**, 2 vols. Pelican Books, ed. V.K. Krishna Memon, 1937.

10. Pinion, F.B. : **A Bronte Companion**, London, 1975.

11. Shorter, Clement & : **The Complete Poems of Emily Jane Bronte**, 1923. C.W. Watfield ed.

12. Spark, Muriel ed. : **The Bronte Letters**, London and New York, 1954.

13. Spark, Muriel and D. Stanford: **Emily Bronte: her life**

and work, London, 1960, Fifth impression, 1975

14. Underhill, Evelyn : **Mysticism**, London, 1911.

15. Willis, Irene Cooper : **The Brontes** : **Great Lives**, London, 1933.

16. Wilson, Romer : **All Alone - The Life and Private History of Emily Jane Bronte**, London, 1928.